Marjoleine's
Letter Cards

Marjolein Zweed

FORTE PUBLISHERS

Contents

ISBN 90 5877 514 3

This is a publication from
Forte Publishers BV
P.O. Box 1394
3500 BJ Utrecht
The Netherlands

For more information about the creative books available from Forte Uitgevers:
www.forteuitgevers.nl

Final editing: Gina Kors-Lambers, Steenwijk, the Netherlands
Photography and digital image editing: Fotografie Gerhard Witteveen, Apeldoorn, the Netherlands
Cover and inner design: BADE creatieve communicatie, Baarn, the Netherlands
Translation: Michael Ford, TextCase, Hilversum, the Netherlands

Preface

People often ask me where I get my ideas for new cards and sheets from. One idea often leads to another, as is the case for this book. My previous book, Marjoleine's Scrapbook, was about creative ways of sticking photographs in photograph albums, for which I designed a number of letter sheets. I have now used these sheets to make greetings cards and the results are shown in this book.

Also as a result of my previous book, I have now used photographs to make cards. The various texts and names which you can add to the cards make them very personal.

Good luck with the cards.

Marjolein

All the cards shown in this book can be found in my shop
Marjolein Zweed Creatief in Abbekerk, the Netherlands.

Techniques

Card and pattern paper
I have used frames made from pattern paper and card on the cards. Since they are slightly different sizes, this produces subtle, narrow borders. Carefully select the card colour, because it is the right colour combination of card, pattern paper and pictures which makes the cards attractive. It is best to cut the card and the pattern paper using a knife and a ruler.

3D pictures
The cards in this book have 3D pictures which are made by sticking several layers of the same picture on top of each other. By placing silicon glue or 3D foam tape between the layers, you create depth and the card becomes three-dimensional.

The cards in this book have been made using two or three layers. You need as many 3D cutting sheets as the number of layers you wish to use. The number of layers used for the cards is stated in each chapter. The cutting patterns used are shown in most of the chapters. Of course, you can always use more or less layers if you wish.

I usually use a knife to cut the straight lines of the pictures and photo glue to stick the first

(bottom) layer on the card. You can use silicon glue or foam tape for the other layers. Try and find out what you prefer, because this is often a personal choice. If you wish, you can first puff up the pictures slightly with your fingers before sticking them on the card.

If you use silicon glue, it is best to put it in a syringe so that it is easier to apply. Apply small drops of silicon glue to the back of the picture and carefully stick the picture on top of the previous picture. Do not press too hard, otherwise you will loose the depth. Do the same for the other layers. You must allow the glue to dry properly before posting the card.

Foam tape can be bought in squares or on a roll which you have to cut into small pieces yourself. Stick the foam tape on the back of the picture and carefully stick the picture on top of the previous picture. Make sure you stick the picture in the right place, because you will not be able to move it about once you have stuck it down. Do the same for the other layers.

Eyelets
Besides normal, round eyelets, there are also many other shapes, such as hearts and stars.

Eyelets are attached to a card using an eyelet toolkit which consists of three different pieces, namely a pipe and two accessories which you can screw onto the pipe. You can use one of the accessories to make a hole and the other accessory, which has a little ball on the end, to secure the eyelets.

When you punch a hole in the card, you must make sure the card is folded open, otherwise there will also be a hole in the back of the card. Place the card on an eyelet mat or an old cutting mat. Never use a good mat, because it will become dented. Place the eyelet tool with the accessory which is used to make holes screwed onto it on the card. Use a hammer to hit the back of the pipe and insert an eyelet through the hole. Place the eyelet tool with the other accessory screwed onto it on the back of the eyelet and use a hammer to hit the back of the pipe again.

Nowadays, there is a toolkit for which you do not require a hammer. The eyelet tool uses a spring. The accessories for making holes and attaching eyelets are the same. If you pull out the cap and then release it, it springs back. By doing this a number of times, you can punch a hole in the card and attach an eyelet (see the step-by-step

photographs). Another tool is the eyelet setter, which splits the back of the eyelet. You can also use the eyelet setter to attach snaps, which are metal circles, to a card (see the card "Paris" on page 15).

Scrapbook Basics
These are small metal shapes which have an eye, so that you can thread a thread through them. If the eye is large enough, you can also attach a Bradletz (small split pen). There is also a piece of foam tape in the packet, which you can use to attach the figure. You can then fold the eye backwards or use a pair of pliers to cut it off.

Step-by-step

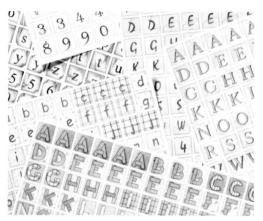

1. Marjoleine's scrapbook paper with letters.

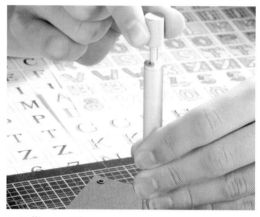

2. Pulling out the cap.

3. Attaching an eyelet.

4. The end result.

Materials

- 3D scissors
- Knife
- Cutting mat
- Transparent cutting ruler (Securit)
- Photo glue
- Silicon glue and a syringe
- Foam tape

- **Marjoleine's 3D cutting sheets**
  Each sheet consists of different squares in a number of different sizes.

- **Marjoleine's pattern paper**
  This series of pattern paper combines very nicely with Marjoleine's 3D cutting sheets.

- **Marjoleine's scrapbook paper**
  You can use this paper to decorate your photograph albums, but as you can see in this book, they can also be used to make cards.

- **Papicolor card**
  You can use this card to make your own cards. You can also buy rectangular and square pre-cut and pre-folded cards. The colour numbers are stated in each chapter.

- **Tools needed for the eyelets**
  Mini eyelet toolkit with a hammer or an eyelet toolkit with a mechanical striker and an eyelet mat.

  The other materials are listed in the chapters in which they are used.

Two-master

25

What you need
- 3D cutting sheet: two-master (2 layers)
- Pattern paper: no. 18
- Scrapbook paper: old alphabet
- Papicolor card:
  light blue (19) and azure (04)

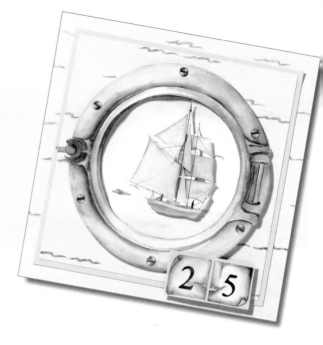

Instructions
1. Take a square, light blue double card
   (13 x 13 cm).

2. Fold a piece of pattern paper (26 x 13 cm)
   double and stick it around the card.

3. Stick a piece of azure card (11.5 x 11.5 cm) and
   a piece of pattern paper (11 x 11 cm) on the
   card.

4. Stick a picture of a porthole (largest size) on
   the top and make it 3D.

5. Use silicon glue or foam tape to stick a boat
   (second largest size) in the porthole.

6. Stick two numbers on azure card and
   cut hem out leaving a small border.

7. Use silicon glue or foam to stick the numbers
   on the card.

Have a good journey

What you need

- *3D cutting sheet: two-master (2 layers)*
- *Pattern paper: no. 18*
- *Scrapbook paper: old alphabet and map*
- *Papicolor card:*
  light blue (19) and azure (04)

Instructions

1. Cut a piece of light blue card (21 x 21 cm) and fold it double.

2. Fold a piece of pattern paper (21 x 21 cm) double and stick it around the card.

3. Stick a piece of azure card (8 x 18 cm) and a piece of pattern paper (7.5 x 17.5 cm) on the card.

4. Stick a map (smallest size) and a picture of a piece of old paper on top.

5. Stick letters and a two-master (smallest size) on the piece of old paper.

6. Stick a picture of a two-master (4 x 4 cm) on the card and make it 3D.

Dirk

What you need
- 3D cutting sheet: two-master (2 layers)
- Pattern paper: no. 18
- Scrapbook paper: old alphabet and map
- Papicolor card:
  light blue (19) and azure (04)
- Scrapbook Basics: sea

Instructions

1. Take a square, light blue double card (13 x 13 cm).

2. Fold a piece of pattern paper (26 x 13 cm) double and stick it around the card.

3. Stick a piece of azure card (10.5 x 10.5 cm) and a piece of pattern paper (10 x 10 cm) on the card.

4. Stick a map and the letters of the person's name on top.

5. Stick a picture of a two-master (3 x 3 cm) on azure card and cut it out leaving a small border.

6. Use silicon glue or foam tape to stick this on the card and make the two-master 3D.

7. Use foam tape to stick a Scrapbook Basic of a lighthouse on the card.

Green letters

50

What you need
- *3D cutting sheet: white roses/anemones (3 layers)*
- *Pattern paper: no. 15*
- *Scrapbook paper: green alphabet, green patchwork and golden brown patchwork*
- *Papicolor card:*
  light green (47) and olive green (45)

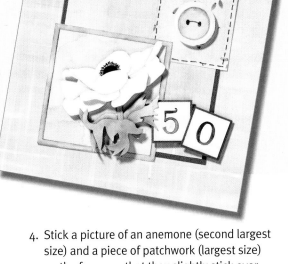

Instructions
1. Take a square, light green double card (13 x 13 cm).

2. Fold a piece of pattern paper (26 x 13 cm) double and stick it around the card.

3. Stick a piece of olive green card (8.5 x 8.5 cm) and a piece of pattern paper (8 x 8 cm) on the card.

4. Stick a picture of an anemone (second largest size) and a piece of patchwork (largest size) on the frame so that they slightly stick over the edge of the frame.

5. Use silicon glue or foam tape to stick a button on the piece of patchwork.

6. Stick two numbers on olive green card and cut them out leaving a small border.

7. Use silicon glue or foam tape to stick the numbers on the card.

8. Make the anemone 3D.

Love

Instructions

1. Take a rectangular, light green double card (10.5 x 15 cm).

2. Fold a piece of pattern paper (15 x 21 cm) double and stick it around the card.

3. Stick a piece of olive green card (2.5 x 15 cm) on the card.

4. Stick a picture of a rose (largest size) on the card and make it 3D.

5. Stick the letters and two tassels on the card. (You can also use a different text, such as "Hurray".)

6. Use silicon glue or foam tape to stick two buttons on the tassels.

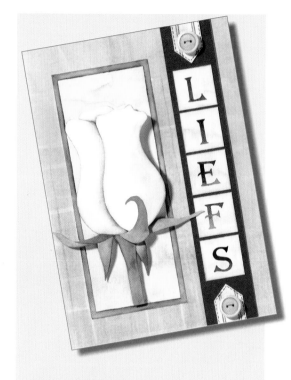

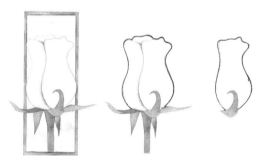

What you need

- *3D cutting sheet: white roses/anemones (3 layers)*
- *Pattern paper: no. 15*
- *Scrapbook paper: green alphabet, green patchwork and golden brown patchwork*
- *Papicolor card:*
  light green (47) and olive green (45)

Hello

Instructions

1. Take a rectangular, light green double card (10.5 x 15 cm).

2. Fold a piece of pattern paper (15 x 21 cm) double and stick it around the card.

3. Cut a 3 cm wide strip off of the front of the card.

4. Stick the letters on the strip which is now visible.

5. Cut out a green label, stick it on olive green card and cut it out leaving a small border.

6. Stick a picture of a tulip (smallest size) on the label.

7. Cut 25 cm of cord, thread it through the label and tie a knot in it.

8. Use silicon glue or foam tape to stick the label on the card.

9. Make the tulip 3D.

What you need

- 3D cutting sheet: white flowers (3 layers)
- Pattern paper: no. 15
- Scrapbook paper: green alphabet and green patchwork
- Papicolor card: olive green (45)
- Waxed cord: natural (2 mm)

Travel

Africa

What you need

- 3D cutting sheet: suitcases (3 layers)
- Scrapbook paper: old alphabet and map
- Papicolor card: nut brown (39) and ice blue (42)
- Scrapbook Basics: travel
- Fun eyelets: antique copper

Instructions

1. Take a rectangular, nut brown double card (10.5 x 15 cm).

2. Stick a piece of ice blue card (9 x 13 cm) and a piece of nut brown card (8.5 x 12.5 cm) on the card.

3. Stick a map (smallest size) and a picture of a piece of old paper on top.

4. Stick letters on the piece of old paper and punch eyelets in it.

5. Stick a picture of a rucksack (3 x 3 cm) on the card and make it 3D.

6. Use foam tape to stick a Scrapbook Basic of a camera on the card.

Paris

What you need

- 3D cutting sheet: suitcases (3 layers)
- Scrapbook paper: old alphabet
- Papicolor card:
  nut brown (39) and dark brown (38)
- Leather corners
- Snaps
- Eyelet setter

Instructions

1. Cut a piece of nut brown card (10.5 x 30 cm).

2. Fold the card double and cut a strip off of the front of the card so that the front measures 10.5 x 10.5 cm.

3. Stick a piece of dark brown card (9 x 9 cm) and a piece of nut brown card (8.5 x 8.5 cm) on the front of the card.

4. Take four leather corners and use the eyelet setter to attach snaps to them.

5. Stick the corners on the card.

6. Stick a picture of a suitcase (largest size), a picture of a rucksack (middle size) and a picture of a pair of shoes (middle size) on the card and make the shoes and the rucksack 3D (2nd and 3rd layers).

7. Stick the letters on the strip which protrudes from the card.

Bon voyage

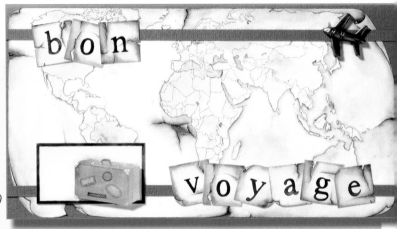

What you need

- 3D cutting sheet: suitcases (2 layers)
- Scrapbook paper: old alphabet and map
- Papicolor card: nut brown (39)
- Scrapbook Basics: travel

Instructions

1. Cut a piece of nut brown card (21 x 21 cm) and fold it double.

2. Stick a map (largest size) on this and cut a 1.5 cm wide strip off of the map so that, after the map has been stuck on the card, a small nut brown border is visible on all sides.

3. Cut two pieces of nut brown card (0.5 x 19.5 cm) and stick them on the card.

4. Stick the letters on the card. (You can also use a different text, such as "Have fun".)

5. Stick a picture of a suitcase (smallest size) on the card and make it 3D.

6. Use foam tape to stick a Scrapbook Basic of an aeroplane on the card. Instead of an aeroplane, you could also use a car, a train or a boat.

Photo cards

Thanks

What you need
- 3D cutting sheet: brown roses (3 layers)
- Pattern paper: no. 12
- Scrapbook paper: old alphabet
- Papicolor card:
  carnation white (03) and nut brown (39)

Instructions
1. Take a square, carnation white double card (13 x 13 cm) and stick a piece of pattern paper (13 x 13 cm) on it.

2. Stick a piece of nut brown card (11 x 11 cm) and a photograph (10.5 x 10.5 cm) on the pattern paper.

3. Stick letters and a picture of a rose (smallest size) on the card.

4. Make the rose 3D.

Hello

Instructions

1. Cut a square (21 x 21 cm) from brick red card and fold it double.

2. Stick a piece of mustard yellow card (7.5 x 11 cm) and a photograph (7 x 10 cm) on the card.

3. Stick the letters and a picture of the autumn leaves (smallest size) on the card.

4. Make the leaf 3D.

What you need

- 3D cutting sheet: autumn leaves (2 layers)
- Scrapbook paper: blue alphabet
- Papicolor card:
  brick red (35) and mustard yellow (48)

Island

Instructions

1. Take a rectangular, night blue double card (10.5 x 15 cm).

2. Fold a piece of pattern paper (15 x 21 cm) double and stick it around the card.

3. Stick a piece of fiesta red card (5.5 x 11 cm) and a photograph (5 x 12 cm) on the card.

4. Stick the letters, a picture of a boat (4 x 4 cm) and a tassel on the card.

5. Make the boat 3D.

6. Use silicon glue or foam tape to stick the buttons on the card.

What you need

- *3D cutting sheet: beach (2 layers)*
- *Pattern paper: no. 16*
- *Scrapbook paper:*
  blue alphabet and blue patchwork
- *Papicolor card:*
  night blue (41) and fiesta red (12)

Rucksack and shoes

4-day walk

What you need

- 3D cutting sheet: suitcases (3 layers)
- Pattern paper: no. 16
- Scrapbook paper: old alphabet and golden brown patchwork
- Papicolor card: night blue (41) and nut brown (39)

Instructions

1. Cut a night blue square (21 x 21 cm) and fold it double.

2. Fold a piece of pattern paper (21 x 21 cm) double and stick it around the card.

3. Stick a piece of nut brown card (7.5 x 17.5 cm) and a piece of pattern paper (7 x 17 cm) on the card.

4. Stick the letters and two tassels on the card.

5. Stick a picture of a pair of shoes and a picture of a rucksack (4 x 4 cm) on the card and make them 3D.

6. Use silicon glue or foam tape to stick the buttons on the tassels.

You've passed your exams

What you need

- 3D cutting sheet: suitcases (3 layers)
- Pattern paper: no. 16
- Scrapbook paper:
  old alphabet and golden brown patchwork
- Papicolor card:
  night blue (41) and dark brown (38)

Instructions

1. Cut a night blue square (21 x 21 cm) and fold it double.

2. Fold a piece of pattern paper (21 x 21 cm) double and stick it around the card.

3. Stick a piece of dark brown card (8 x 18 cm) and a piece of pattern paper (7.5 x 17.5 cm) on the card.

4. Stick a picture of a rucksack (6 x 6 cm) on top and make it 3D.

5. Stick the letters and a tassel on the card.

6. Use silicon glue or foam tape to stick a button on the tassel.

Hello

What you need

- 3D cutting sheet: suitcases (3 layers)
- Pattern paper: no. 16
- Scrapbook paper: old alphabet
- Papicolor card: nut brown (39)
- Fun eyelets: antique copper
- Waxed cord: natural (1 mm)

Instructions

1. Cut a piece of nut brown card (10.5 x 30 cm) and a piece of pattern paper (10.5 x 30 cm).

2. Score the nut brown card 10.5 cm and 25.5 cm from one end and fold it.

3. Stick the piece of pattern paper around the card. Leave a small nut brown border at the beginning, continue at the back and go to the front again.

4. Cut a small piece off of the pattern paper, if necessary, to make sure there is a small nut brown border at the end.

5. Stick a picture of a pair of shoes (largest size) on the front of the card and make it 3D.

6. Stick letters on the narrow side of the card.

7. Punch four eyelets in each side of the card, 1.5 cm from the top and bottom of the card and 2.5 cm apart.

8. Cut 80 cm of cord and thread it through the eyelets like a lace.

Daisies

65

What you need
- *3D cutting sheet: daisies (3 layers)*
- *Pattern paper: no. 17*
- *Scrapbook paper:*
  blue alphabet and blue patchwork
- *Papicolor card: night blue (41)*
- *Waxed cord: natural (2 mm)*

Instructions
1. Take a square, night blue double card (13 x 13 cm).

2. Fold a piece of pattern paper (26 x 13 cm) double and stick it around the card.

3. Stick a piece of night blue card (10.5 x 10.5 cm) and a piece of pattern paper (10 x 10 cm) on the card.

4. Cut out a blue label, stick it on night blue card and cut it out leaving a small border.

5. Stick a picture of a daisy (smallest size) on the label.

6. Cut 25 cm of cord, thread it through the label and tie a knot in it.

7. Use silicon glue or foam tape to stick the label on the card.

8. Make the daisy 3D.

9. Stick two numbers on night blue card and cut them out leaving a small border.

10. Use silicon glue or foam tape to stick the numbers on the card.

Hello

Instructions

1. Take a rectangular, night blue double card (10.5 x 15 cm).

2. Fold a piece of pattern paper (15 x 21 cm) double and stick it around the card.

3. Cut a 3 cm wide strip off of the front of the card.

4. Stick the letters on the strip which protrudes from the card.

5. Cut out a picture of a daisy (largest size). Stick it on night blue card and cut it out leaving a small border.

6. Punch eyelets in the corners and stick it on the card.

7. Make the daisy 3D.

What you need
- *3D cutting sheet: daisies (3 layers)*
- *Pattern paper: no. 17*
- *Scrapbook paper: blue alphabet*
- *Papicolor card: night blue (41)*
- *Fun eyelets: dark blue*

Instructions

1. Take a rectangular, night blue double card (10.5 x 15 cm).

2. Fold a piece of pattern paper (15 x 21 cm) double and stick it around the card.

3. Stick a piece of night blue card (4 x 15 cm) 1 cm from the side of the card.

4. Stick three pictures of a daisy (smallest size) on the strip and make them 3D.

5. Stick two numbers on the card.

What you need

- 3D cutting sheet: daisies (3 layers)
- Pattern paper: no. 17
- Scrapbook paper: blue alphabet
- Papicolor card: night blue (41)

Fish

5

What you need
- *Pattern paper: no. 18*
- *Scrapbook paper: bright letters and fish*
- *Papicolor card: turquoise (32)*

Instructions

1. Cut a piece of turquoise card (10.5 x 30 cm) and a piece of pattern paper no. 18 (10.5 x 30 cm).

2. Fold the piece of card double and cut a strip off of the front of the card so that the front measures 10.5 x 10.5 cm.

3. Stick the piece of pattern paper around the card. Start where you just cut the front off and leave a small turquoise border. Continue at the back and go to the front again.

4. Use silicon glue or foam tape to stick a picture of a fish (largest size) and some buttons on the front of the card.

5. Use silicon glue or foam tape to stick a number and two buttons on the strip which protrudes from the card.

6. Stick part of a tassel on the card and fold the excess behind the card.

7. Use silicon glue or foam tape to stick a button on the tassel.

Summer

What you need
- *Pattern paper: no. 17*
- *Scrapbook paper: bright letters and fish*
- *Papicolor card:*
  violet (20) and iris blue (31)
- *White gel pen*

Instructions
1. Take a rectangular, violet double card (10.5 x 15 cm).

2. Stick a piece of iris blue card (12.5 x 8.5 cm) and a piece of pattern paper no. 17 (12 x 8 cm) on the card.

3. Stick pieces of patchwork and letters on the card.

4. Stick a piece of iris blue card (6 x 4 cm) on the card and use the white gel pen to draw stitches around the edge.

5. Use silicon glue or foam tape to stick a picture of a fish (smallest size) on it.

6. Use silicon glue or foam tape to stick some buttons and a picture of the sun on the card.

Hurray!

What you need
- *Pattern paper: no. 18*
- *Scrapbook paper:*
  bright letters and fish
- *Papicolor card:*
  light blue (19) and iris blue (31)

Instructions

1. Take a rectangular, light blue double card (10.5 x 15 cm).

2. Fold a piece of pattern paper no. 18 (15 x 21 cm) double and stick it around the card.

3. Stick a strip of light blue card (2.5 x 15 cm) 1 cm from the bottom of the card.

4. Use silicon glue or foam tape to stick two buttons on the strip. The exclamation mark is the letter "i" turned upside down.

5. Use silicon glue or foam tape to stick two fish on the card.

Bears

Jet

What you need
- 3D cutting sheet: pink teddy bears (3 layers)
- Pattern paper: no. 13
- Scrapbook paper: patchwork alphabet and pink ducks
- Papicolor card: pale pink (23) and cerise (33)

Instructions

1. Take a rectangular, pale pink double card (10.5 x 15 cm).

2. Fold a piece of pattern paper no. 13 (15 x 21 cm) double and stick it around the card.

3. Stick a piece of cerise card (6.5 x 6.5 cm) on the card.

4. Stick three letters, two small pieces of patchwork and a picture of two bears (4 x 4 cm) on top.

5. Stick a safety pin on the card.

6. Use silicon glue or foam tape to stick a button on one of the pieces of patchwork.

7. Make the bears 3D.

Baby

Instructions

1. Take a square, lavender double card (13 x 13 cm) and stick a piece of pattern paper no. 7 (13 x 13 cm) on it.

2. Stick a picture of a bear on the card and make it 3D.

3. Stick the letters on night blue card and cut them out leaving a small border. (Instead of the word "Baby", you could also write the name of the baby.)

4. Use silicon glue or foam tape to stick the letters on the card.

5. Use foam tape to stick a Scrapbook Basic of a safety pin on the card.

What you need

- *3D cutting sheet: blue teddy bears (3 layers)*
- *Pattern paper: no. 7*
- *Scrapbook paper: brown alphabet*
- *Papicolor card:*
  lavender (21) and night blue (41)
- *Scrapbook Basics: baby*

3 years old

Instructions

1. Take a rectangular, carnation white double card (10.5 x 15 cm) and cut 1.5 cm off of it.

2. Fold a piece of pattern paper no. 7 (18 x 15 cm) double and stick it around the card.

3. Stick a piece of night blue card (6.5 x 12.5 cm) on the card.

4. Stick the letters and a picture of some bears on top.

5. Make the bears 3D.

6. Use foam tape to stick a Scrapbook Basic of a rocking horse on the card.

What you need

- 3D cutting sheet: blue teddy bears
- Pattern paper: no. 7
- Scrapbook paper: patchwork alphabet
- Papicolor card:
  carnation white (03) and night blue (41)
- Scrapbook Basics: baby

Cards on the cover

25

What you need
- 3D cutting sheet: two-master (2 layers)
- Scrapbook paper: old alphabet
- Papicolor card: nut brown (39) and ice blue (42)

Instructions
1. Cut a piece of nut brown card (10.5 x 30 cm).

2. Fold the card double and cut a strip off of the front of the card so that the front measures 10.5 x 10.5 cm.

3. Stick a piece of ice blue card (9 x 9 cm) and a piece of nut brown card (8.5 x 8.5 cm) on the front of the card.

4. Stick a picture of a porthole (smallest size) on top and make it 3D.

5. Use silicon glue or foam tape to stick a boat (second smallest size) in the porthole.

6. Stick two numbers on the strip which protrudes from the card.

Congratulations

What you need
- 3D cutting sheet: two-master (2 layers)
- Scrapbook paper: old alphabet and map
- Papicolor card: nut brown (39) and ice blue (42)

Instructions
1. Take a square, ice blue double card (13 x 13 cm).

2. Stick a piece of nut brown card (11.5 x 11.5 cm) and a piece of ice blue card (11 x 11 cm) on the card.

3. Stick a map (smallest size) and the letters on top.

4. Stick a picture of a two-master (4 x 4 cm) on top and make it 3D.

The materials used can be ordered by shopkeepers from: Kars & Co BV in Ochten, the Netherlands
• Jalekro B.V. in Assendelft, the Netherlands
• Papicolor International B.V. in Utrecht, the Netherlands • Vadeko Kreatief in Spijkenisse, the Netherlands • HOCA in Beek en Donk, the Netherlands